QUIZ WHIZ

QUIZ PACK 1

HAPPY HOLIDAYS!

1 True or false? The Chinese New Year always takes place on January 1.

2 Which of these trees is most often used as a Christmas tree?

a. fir   c. palm
b. birch   d. weeping willow

3 True or false? Each November, a town in Thailand prepares a special feast for local wild monkeys.

4 About how many turkeys are eaten each year on Thanksgiving?

a. 1 million   c. 20 million
b. 5 million   d. 45 million

5 In what country do people celebrate the Day of the Dead?

a. Ireland   c. Mexico
b. Japan   d. Morocco

6 True or false? A shamrock, worn by many people on St. Patrick's Day, is a four-leaf clover.

7 Which vegetable was used to make Halloween jack-o'-lanterns, before people started using pumpkins?

a. spinach   c. carrots
b. celery   d. turnips

8 According to legend, what happens if a groundhog sees its shadow on Groundhog Day?

a. there will be six more weeks of winter
b. spring has officially begun
c. there will be no summer
d. winter will last all year

9 In 2011, the most popular Halloween costume for pets was a ____.

a. pumpkin
b. hot dog
c. pirate
d. ghost

10 Rio de Janeiro, Brazil, is famous for its celebration of _____, during which thousands of people in **costumes** parade through the streets.

a. Carnival
b. St. Patrick's Day
c. Christmas
d. Presidents' Day

11 During the Jewish holiday **Hanukkah,** kids receive gifts of chocolate candies that are shaped like what?

a. menorahs
b. flowers
c. stars
d. coins

12 Which holiday—celebrated from December 26 to January 1—means **"first fruits"** in the African language called Swahili?

a. Ramadan
b. Christmas
c. Kwanzaa
d. New Year's Day

13 On **May Day,** children in England welcome spring by dancing around what?

a. a chocolate fountain
b. a piñata
c. a maypole
d. a bean stalk

14 If all of the candy conversation hearts made every year—sold mostly for Valentine's Day—were lined up, how far would they stretch?

a. ten city blocks
b. around the Earth
c. to the moon
d. across the United States twice

CHECK YOUR ANSWERS ON PAGES 22–23.

GRAND CANYON ADVENTURE

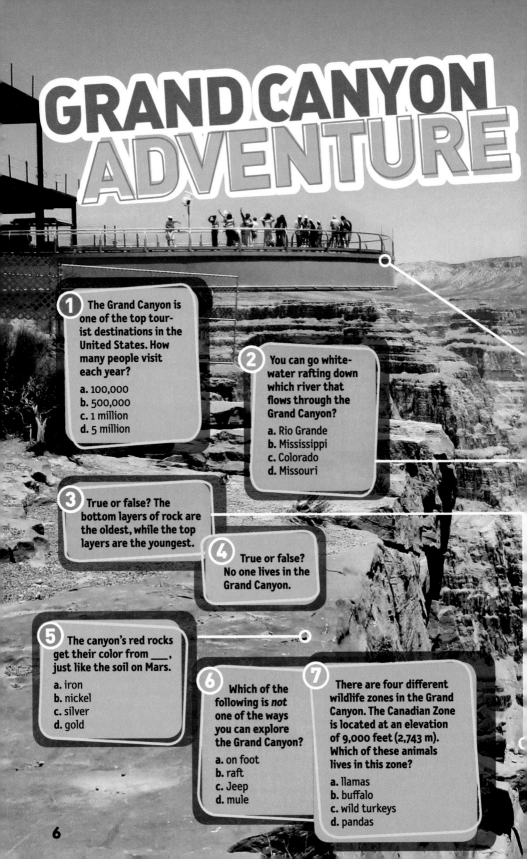

1 The Grand Canyon is one of the top tourist destinations in the United States. How many people visit each year?

a. 100,000
b. 500,000
c. 1 million
d. 5 million

2 You can go white-water rafting down which river that flows through the Grand Canyon?

a. Rio Grande
b. Mississippi
c. Colorado
d. Missouri

3 True or false? The bottom layers of rock are the oldest, while the top layers are the youngest.

4 True or false? No one lives in the Grand Canyon.

5 The canyon's red rocks get their color from ___, just like the soil on Mars.

a. iron
b. nickel
c. silver
d. gold

6 Which of the following is *not* one of the ways you can explore the Grand Canyon?

a. on foot
b. raft
c. Jeep
d. mule

7 There are four different wildlife zones in the Grand Canyon. The Canadian Zone is located at an elevation of 9,000 feet (2,743 m). Which of these animals lives in this zone?

a. llamas
b. buffalo
c. wild turkeys
d. pandas

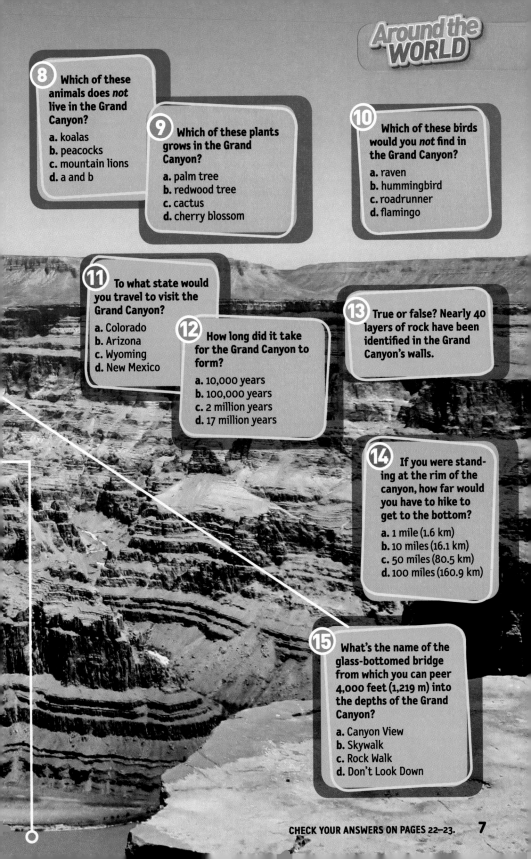

8 Which of these animals does *not* live in the Grand Canyon?

a. koalas
b. peacocks
c. mountain lions
d. a and b

9 Which of these plants grows in the Grand Canyon?

a. palm tree
b. redwood tree
c. cactus
d. cherry blossom

10 Which of these birds would you *not* find in the Grand Canyon?

a. raven
b. hummingbird
c. roadrunner
d. flamingo

11 To what state would you travel to visit the Grand Canyon?

a. Colorado
b. Arizona
c. Wyoming
d. New Mexico

12 How long did it take for the Grand Canyon to form?

a. 10,000 years
b. 100,000 years
c. 2 million years
d. 17 million years

13 True or false? Nearly 40 layers of rock have been identified in the Grand Canyon's walls.

14 If you were standing at the rim of the canyon, how far would you have to hike to get to the bottom?

a. 1 mile (1.6 km)
b. 10 miles (16.1 km)
c. 50 miles (80.5 km)
d. 100 miles (160.9 km)

15 What's the name of the glass-bottomed bridge from which you can peer 4,000 feet (1,219 m) into the depths of the Grand Canyon?

a. Canyon View
b. Skywalk
c. Rock Walk
d. Don't Look Down

What's on THE MENU?

① **True or false?** Scorpions are considered a tasty treat in China.

② If you ordered brat-wurst in Germany, you'd be asking for what kind of food?
- a. pretzel
- b. sausage
- c. cake
- d. fruit

③ You may want to pinch your nose while eating durian, a fruit from Southeast Asia. The smell of durian has been compared to what?
- a. turpentine
- b. a campground toilet
- c. rotting fish
- d. all of the above

④ If you walked into a McDon-ald's in Norway, you'd find a McLacks on the menu. What's a McLacks? (Hint: "Lacks" is pronounced like "lox.")
- a. a salmon burger
- b. a turkey burger
- c. a veggie burger
- d. a regular hamburger

⑤ In the United States, some people eat turducken instead of a traditional turkey for Thanksgiving. What is this dish?
- a. a vegetarian turkey made of soybeans
- b. tofu lasagna
- c. duck stew
- d. a chicken stuffed into a duck stuffed into a turkey

⑥ Which country is the world's leading banana grower?
- a. United States
- b. India
- c. Denmark
- d. Argentina

(7) **True or false?** "Swiss cheese" is always made in Switzerland.

(8) **True or false?** Modern-day pizza was inspired by the colors of the Italian flag.

(9) **What food was named for the rolled packs that** *burros* **(the Spanish word for donkeys) often carried on their backs in Mexico?**

a. enchilada
b. taco
c. burrito
d. nachos

(10) **In Jamaica, the word "jerk" is used to describe what?**

a. a type of candy
b. spiced and grilled meat
c. a crop of plantains
d. a mean person

(11) **The deep-fried Mars bar was created in what country?**

a. United States
b. Kenya
c. Scotland
d. Spain

(12) **Which is not the name of an English food?**

a. bubble and squeak
b. parson's nose
c. candyfloss
d. potter pie

CHECK YOUR ANSWERS ON PAGES 22–23.

The Wide WORLD OF SPORTS

1 One of the world's most popular sports is known as "soccer" in Australia, Canada, New Zealand, and the U.S. But what is it called in most other countries?

a. kickball
b. goalkeeper
c. World Cup
d. football

2 **True or false?** Each of the five Olympic rings is a different color to represent the five major regions of the world involved in the Olympics.

3 What is the name of the sport, popular in both Canada and Scotland, that involves a broom?

a. ice hockey
b. lacrosse
c. sweeping
d. curling

4 **True or false?** In Afghanistan, the sport of kite fighting involves cutting your opponents' kite strings so that your kite can fly the highest and longest.

5 The tropical island nation of Jamaica surprised the world when it took part in what sport in the 1988 Winter Olympics?

a. swimming
b. running
c. bobsledding
d. water polo

6 The world's heaviest sumo wrestler weighed 630 pounds (287 kg). That's almost as heavy as a male _____.

a.
brown bear

b.
sheep

c.
blue whale

d.
golden retriever

CHECK YOUR ANSWERS ON PAGES 22–23.

(7) There are ten different sports in a decathlon. Which of the following is not a decathlon sport?

a. long jump
b. pole vault
c. marathon
d. javelin throw

(8) Which American football team won the first ever Super Bowl, played in 1967?

a. Green Bay Packers
b. Dallas Cowboys
c. New Orleans Saints
d. Kansas City Chiefs

(9) This skateboarder, nick-named "The Birdman," was the first ever to land a trick called the 900—that's two and a half turns in the air!

a. Shaun White
b. Andy Macdonald
c. Tony Hawk
d. Ryan Sheckler

(10) Which country has won the most Olympic medals?

a. Italy
b. United States
c. Germany
d. Greece

(11) What is the name of the instrument that fans could be heard blowing during the 2010 FIFA World Cup?

a. harmonica
b. bullhorn
c. trumpet
d. vuvuzela

(12) True or false? In Malaysia, some athletes play tennis using their legs and feet instead of racquets.

TRUE or FALSE?
Dream Vacations

1. YOU'D HAVE TO CLIMB 354 STEPS TO REACH THE TOP OF THE STATUE OF LIBERTY.

2. IN SWEDEN, YOU CAN STAY IN A HOTEL MADE OF ICE.

3. *ALOHA* MEANS "HELLO" AND "GOODBYE" IN THE HAWAIIAN LANGUAGE.

4. SIX FLAGS DOES *NOT* HAVE A SITE IN FLORIDA, U.S.A.

5. IF YOU WERE IN JAPAN, YOU WOULD PAY FOR YOUR MEAL WITH A EURO.

6. THE FAMOUS CLOCK TOWER IN LONDON, ENGLAND, IS NICKNAMED "BIG BEN."

7. THE LEANING TOWER IN PISA, ITALY, BEGAN TO TILT BEFORE CONSTRUCTION OF THE BUILDING HAD EVEN BEEN COMPLETED.

8. THE CHEESEHEAD HAT—A POPULAR SOUVENIR IN WISCONSIN, U.S.A.—WAS FIRST MADE OF REAL CHEDDAR CHEESE.

9. LAS VEGAS IS HOME TO A GROUP OF SKYDIVING ELVIS IMPERSONATORS CALLED THE "FLYING ELVI."

10. AN IMAGE OF A JAGUAR APPEARS ON CANADA'S MONEY.

11. JAPAN IS HOME TO THE WORLD'S LARGEST FISH MARKET.

12. THERE'S A HOTEL MADE ENTIRELY OF SAND IN WEYMOUTH BEACH IN ENGLAND, U.K.

13. THE WORLD'S BIGGEST FOOD FIGHT TAKES PLACE EACH SUMMER IN SPAIN.

14. STONEHENGE, A PREHISTORIC STONE MONUMENT IN ENGLAND, U.K., WAS USED AS A CLOCK WHEN IT WAS FIRST BUILT.

15. THERE'S A TOILET-SHAPED ROCK MONUMENT IN NEW MEXICO, U.S.A.

16 THE WORLD'S MOST EXPENSIVE HOTEL SUITE COSTS $65,000 A NIGHT.

17 LLANFAIRPWLLGWYNGYLLGOGERYCHWYRNDROBWLLLLANTYSILIOGOGOGOCH IS THE NAME OF A VILLAGE IN WALES, U.K.

18 THE FACES OF THREE U.S. PRESIDENTS ARE CHISELED INTO THE SIDE OF MOUNT RUSHMORE IN NORTH DAKOTA, U.S.A.

19 THE WORLD'S TALLEST BRIDGE IS SO HIGH THAT MOTORISTS CAN DRIVE THROUGH THE CLOUDS.

20 THE ITALIAN CITY OF VENICE, WHICH ATTRACTS 20 MILLION TOURISTS EACH YEAR, IS SLOWLY SINKING.

21 DISNEYLAND IN CALIFORNIA, U.S.A., IS HOME TO THE EPCOT THEME PARK.

22 THE GREAT BARRIER REEF—A CORAL REEF SYSTEM IN AUSTRALIA— CAN BE SEEN FROM SPACE.

23 THE ORIENT EXPRESS WAS THE NAME OF A PASSENGER TRAIN THAT ORIGINALLY RAN FROM FRANCE TO ROMANIA.

24 CALIFORNIA'S REDWOOD FOREST HAS TREES THAT ARE TALLER THAN THE STATUE OF LIBERTY IN NEW YORK, U.S.A.

25 YOU CAN TAKE A BATH IN A TUB OF RAMEN NOODLES IN JAPAN.

26 LEGEND HAS IT THAT IF YOU KISS THE BLARNEY STONE IN IRELAND, U.K., YOU'LL HAVE THE "GIFT OF GAB."

27 YOU CAN TAKE A VACATION TO THE SOUTH POLE.

28 THE "MONA LISA," LOCATED IN THE LOUVRE MUSEUM IN PARIS, FRANCE, IS CONSIDERED TO BE THE WORLD'S MOST EXPENSIVE PAINTING.

29 THE FAMOUS HOLLYWOOD SIGN IN LOS ANGELES, CALIFORNIA, U.S.A., READ "HOLLYWOODLAND" WHEN IT WAS FIRST CREATED.

30 EVERYTHING IN THE RED SQUARE IN MOSCOW, RUSSIA, IS RED.

Earthly EXTREMES

1 This destination gets more than 52 feet (16 m) of snow each year, making it the snowiest place on Earth.

    a. the North Pole
    b. Mount Rainier, Washington, U.S.A.
    c. Whistler, British Columbia, Canada
    d. Antarctica

2 What is the world's longest river?

    a. the Mississippi in the United States
    b. the Yangtze in China
    c. the Amazon in South America
    d. the Nile in Africa

3 In Longyearbyen, Norway—the world's northernmost town—the sun does not rise for how long?

    a. 24 hours
    b. one week
    c. one month
    d. four months

4 True or false? The ocean's deepest trench is deeper than Mount Everest is high.

5 Sandboarders flock to Peru because the country has the world's tallest _____.

    a. snowbanks
    b. sand dunes
    c. waves
    d. anthills

6 The hottest known temperature on Earth was recorded in El Azizia, Libya. How hot was it?

a. 119°F (48°C)
b. 136°F (58°C)
c. 223°F (106°C)
d. 275°F (135°C)

7 The world's largest desert, the Sahara in Africa, is about the size of _____?

a. Rome, Italy
b. Puerto Rico
c. the Amazon rain forest
d. Australia

SAHARA

8 Surfers have been traveling to Nazare, Portugal, to ride some of the world's tallest waves. In 2011, surfer Garrett McNamara rode a wave that was how tall?

a. 10 feet (3 m)
b. 20 feet (6 m)
c. 50 feet (15 m)
d. 90 feet (27 m)

9 The world's deepest cave, in Ukraine, is 6,824 feet (2,080 m) from top to bottom. That's about the same as the height of _____.

a. two Eiffel Towers (Paris, France)
b. the Washington Monument (Washington, D.C., U.S.A.)
c. the Tower of Pisa (Pisa, Italy)
d. five Empire State Buildings (New York, N.Y., U.S.A.)

10 **True or false?** It's impossible to sink in Israel's Dead Sea.

11 The world's highest waterfall (shown at right) is _____ in Venezuela.

a. Niagara Falls
b. Iguazu Falls
c. Victoria Falls
d. Angel Falls

CHECK YOUR ANSWERS ON PAGES 22–23.

BE POLITE AROUND THE GLOBE

1 If you want **to greet** someone in **Tibet**, you can ____.

a. stick out your tongue
b. brush your hair
c. spin around
d. scream

2 In **England**, people often do this when they don't like a performer.

a. clap slowly
b. laugh
c. whistle
d. stay in their seats

3 It is customary for people in **Morocco** to offer their guests what?

a. mint tea
b. handmade rugs
c. pine nuts
d. camels

4 In **Bulgaria**, which of these gestures means "yes"?

a. nodding your head
b. shaking your head
c. smiling
d. running in place

5 In the **Czech Republic**, what do wedding guests often throw at a newly married couple?

a. rice
b. peas
c. flowers
d. rocks

6 In **Japan**, what is it polite to do before entering someone's house?

a. knock on the door three times
b. put on a hat
c. take off your shoes
d. jump up and down

7 In **Holland**, it is polite to eat your bread in what way?

a. with your hands
b. with chopsticks
c. with a knife and fork
d. with your feet

8 In Indonesia, what body part should you use to point to something?

a. thumb
b. elbow
c. index finger
d. foot

9 People in Switzerland think it's gross to do what in public?

a. speak
b. hold hands
c. chew gum
d. kiss

10 True or false? In China, it is considered rude to eat everything on your plate.

11 True or false? In Turkey, a strong handshake is considered impolite.

12 What number is considered lucky in Italy?

a. 3
b. 7
c. 13
d. 21

13 In what country is it rude to make eye contact when you greet someone?

a. Spain
b. Denmark
c. United States
d. China

14 In Taiwan, it's polite to do what if you enjoyed your meal?

a. rub your belly
b. smile
c. burp
d. take a nap

MAP MANIA!
WONDERS OF THE WORLD

① TAJ MAHAL

Made entirely from white marble, the Taj Mahal was built by the emperor Shah Jahan for what reason?

a. to honor his deceased wife
b. to honor his children
c. to please his king
d. to create a tourist attraction in his country

② COLOSSEUM

The Colosseum is an arena that held up to 50,000 spectators. People often came to watch fierce fighters called _____.

a. Vikings
b. barbarians
c. gladiators
d. avatars

③ CHRIST THE REDEEMER STATUE

What is the name of the mountain on which the Christ the Redeemer statue stands?

a. Mount Everest
b. Kilimanjaro
c. Corcovado
d. Mount Olympus

④ CHICHÉN ITZÁ

At certain times of year, the sunset casts shadows on this famous Mayan pyramid, creating the appearance of what kind of animal slithering down its stairs?

a. jaguar
b. lizard
c. lion
d. snake

NORTH AMERICA

MEXICO

A

SOUTH AMERICA

PERU

BRAZIL

B

C

You'd have to travel the globe to visit all of the New 7 Wonders of the World, voted on in a worldwide poll. Take this quick tour to find out how much you know about these man-made marvels. Then try to match each one to the correct location on the map.

⑤ GREAT WALL

The world's longest structure ever made by humans, the Great Wall stretches about how far?

a. 100 miles (161 km)
b. 1,000 miles (1,609 km)
c. 4,500 miles (7,242 km)
d. 10,000 miles (16,093 km)

⑥ MACHU PICCHU

True or false? Inca workers moved giant stones up the 7,970-foot-tall (2,429 m) mountain shown below to build Machu Picchu.

EUROPE
D.
ITALY
A
CHINA G
JORDAN
E
F
INDIA
AFRICA
AUSTRALIA
ANTARCTICA

⑦ PETRA

This ancient city is carved into a cliff made of which natural material?

a. ivory
b. sandstone
c. gold
d. diamonds

⑧-⑭ THE COUNTRIES HIGHLIGHTED

IN ORANGE ON THE MAP ARE EACH HOME TO ONE OF THESE WONDERS. MATCH EACH WONDER TO THE RED MARKER THAT SHOWS ITS CORRECT LOCATION.

CHECK YOUR ANSWERS ON PAGES 22–23.

GAME SHOW
ULTIMATE GLOBAL CHALLENGE

1 Where can you find this famous building?

a. Moscow, Russia
b. Rome, Italy
c. Sydney, Australia
d. Jerusalem, Israel

2 Which country has the most people?
a. the United States
b. Russia
c. China
d. Mexico

3 TRUE OR FALSE?
San Francisco's Golden Gate Bridge is painted gold.

4 There are more countries on this continent than any other.
a. Europe
b. Africa
c. Asia
d. South America

5 On what holiday is it traditional to eat corned beef and cabbage?
a. Valentine's Day
b. St. Patrick's Day
c. April Fool's Day
d. Thanksgiving

6 During a famous festival in Pamplona, Spain, thousands of people are chased through the city streets by what?
a. Spanish dancers
b. kangaroos
c. bulls
d. monster trucks

7 Which skyscraper is the tallest in the world?
a. Taipei 101 in Taipei, Taiwan
b. Petronas Towers in Kuala Lumpur, Malaysia
c. Willis Tower in Chicago, Illinois, U.S.A.
d. Burj Khalifa, in Dubai, United Arab Emirates

8 "The Big Apple" is a nickname for which city?
a. Moscow, Russia
b. New York, New York, U.S.A.
c. London, England, U.K.
d. Hong Kong, China

9 Neuschwanstein Castle in Bavaria, Germany, was the inspiration for which of these storybook locations?
a. Hogwarts School of Witchcraft and Wizardry
b. Sleeping Beauty Castle in Disneyland
c. Dracula's Castle
d. Emerald City in the Wizard of Oz

10 What sport was invented in Scotland?
a. baseball
b. basketball
c. snowboarding
d. golf

11 The hundred highest mountains in the world are all on which continent?
a. North America
b. Africa
c. Asia
d. Antarctica

12 TRUE OR FALSE?
There is a heart-shaped coral reef in Australia.

13 Which monument was a gift to the United States from France?

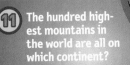
a. Statue of Liberty
b. Lincoln Memorial

c. Iwo Jima Monument
d. Paul Bunyan Statue

14 Which of the following would you not see in Amsterdam, Holland?
a. tulips
b. windmills
c. canals
d. a mountain range

15 ULTIMATE BRAIN BUSTER

IN WHICH OF THESE FAMOUS PLACES DOES THE QUEEN OF ENGLAND LIVE?

a. St. Basil's Cathedral
b. White House
c. Buckingham Palace
d. Tower Bridge

ANSWERS

Happy Holidays!, pages 4–5

1. **False.** Chinese New Year can take place in January or February, because it's based on the Chinese, or Yin, calendar.
2. **a**
3. **True.** At the annual Monkey Buffet Festival, the people of Lopburi, Thailand, honor 2,000 long-tailed macaques that live nearby. Locals believe the monkeys bring good fortune.
4. **d**
5. **c**
6. **False.** A shamrock is a three-leaf clover, a shape often worn as a symbol of Ireland. A four-leaf clover is said to bring good luck.
7. **d**
8. **a**
9. **a**
10. **a**
11. **d**
12. **c**
13. **c**
14. **d**

Grand Canyon Adventure, pages 6–7

1. **d**
2. **c**
3. **True.** The canyon is made from sedimentary rocks deposited in layers by wind or water. The bottom layers were the first to be deposited; the top layers were the last.
4. **False.** Native American tribes, including the Hualapi, Havasupai, and Navajo live on reservations in the Grand Canyon.
5. **a**
6. **c**
7. **c**
8. **d**
9. **c**
10. **d**
11. **b**
12. **d**
13. **True.** Some layers are made of sand, lime, or mud that hardened into rock.
14. **a**
15. **b**

What's on the Menu? pages 8–9

1. **True.** Deep-fried scorpions sprinkled with spices are considered a delicacy in China.
2. **b**
3. **d**
4. **a**
5. **d**
6. **b**
7. **False.** Swiss cheese is actually made in the United States and Canada. It resembles a cheese from Switzerland called Emmentaler.
8. **True.** The first pizza was served to Queen Margherita of Italy. It was

made with white cheese, green basil, and red tomato.
9. **c**
10. **b**
11. **c**
12. **d**

The Wide World of Sports, pages 10–11

1. **d**
2. **True.** Blue represents Europe, yellow represents Asia, black represents Africa, green represents Oceania, and red represents the Americas.
3. **d**
4. **True.** Players use sharp objects in their kites to cut their opponents' kite strings.
5. **c**
6. **a**
7. **c**
8. **a**
9. **c**
10. **b**
11. **d**
12. **True.** In Malaysia, "foot tennis" involves passing a ball across a net using the feet, knees, and thighs.

True or False? Dream Vacations, pages 12–13

1. **True.** If you're up for the climb, you can check out the view from the statue's crown.
2. **True.** Sweden's Icehotel even has beds made of ice and snow.
3. **True.** "Aloha" has many different meanings in Hawaiian.
4. **True.** However, Disney, SeaWorld, and Universal Studios do have theme parks in Florida.
5. **False.** The yen is the currency of Japan.
6. **False.** The nickname actually refers to the 13.5-ton bell inside the clock tower, not the clock tower itself.
7. **True.** Because the tower had been built on unstable ground, part of it began to lean as workers were beginning construction on the second floor.
8. **False.** The first cheesehead hat was made of couch foam.
9. **True.** In addition to the "Flying Elvi," Las Vegas is home to big Elvises, little Elvises, female Elvises, and Elvis waiters, ministers, and chefs.
10. **False.** Only animals native to Canada appear on Canada's currency—such as the beaver, the caribou, and the polar bear. The jaguar appears on the currency of Brazil, where these big cats live in the wild.
11. **True.** The Tsukiji Market is in Tokyo, Japan. More than 900 vendors sell more than 400 different types of seafood.
12. **True.** Weymouth Beach Sand Castle Hotel is made up of 2,200,000 pounds (1 million kg) of sand.
13. **True.** During a festival called La Toma-

tina, thousands of people hurl 120 tons of tomatoes at each other in the streets of Buñol, Spain.
14. **False.** No one's really sure why Stonehenge was built. Some researchers think it was either a place of healing or a monument to honor the dead.
15. **True.** Toilet Rock is in City of Rocks State Park in Faywood, New Mexico.
16. **True.** The hotel suite, at the Hotel President Wilson in Geneva, Switzerland, has 12 rooms and costs more than some luxury cars.
17. **True.** The name of the village means "Saint Mary's Church in a hollow of white hazel near the swirling whirlpool of the church of Saint Tysilio with a red cave" in Welsh.
18. **False.** The faces of four U.S. Presidents—George Washington, Abraham Lincoln, Theodore Roosevelt, and Thomas Jefferson—are sculpted into the mountainside.
19. **True.** The roadway of the Millau Viaduct bridge in France is 885 feet (270 m) high.
20. **True.** Venice is built in a lagoon. The city has sunk 10 inches (25 cm) in the last 100 years.
21. **False.** Epcot is located at Walt Disney World in Florida, U.S.A.
22. **True.** The Great Barrier Reef spans 1,600 miles (2,600 km) and is large enough to be seen from the International Space Station.
23. **True.** The train first ran from Paris, France to Giurgiu, Romania.
24. **True.** The forest contains the world's tallest tree, at 379 feet (116 m). The Statue of Liberty is 305 feet (93 m) from base to torch.
25. **True.** A Ramen noodle bath is available to customers at Yunessan Spa in Japan.
26. **True.** Kissing the Blarney Stone is said to make you a great and flattering speaker.
27. **True.** There are no hotels at the South Pole, but you can take a cruise to Antarctica and a guided tour of the pole.
28. **True.** Though the "Mona Lisa" has not been sold, experts say that it is worth more than $670 million.
29. **True.** The sign was created in 1923 as an advertisement for a new housing development. The last four letters were removed in 1949.
30. **False.** The word "red" came from a word that once meant "beautiful" in Russian.

Earthly Extremes, pages 14–15

1. **b**
2. **d**
3. **d**
4. **True.** The Challenger Deep, located in the Mariana Trench in the Pacific Ocean, is almost seven miles (11 km) deep. If Mount Everest were placed inside, there would still be more than 6,000 feet (1,829 m) of water above it.
5. **b**
6. **b**
7. **d**

8. d
9. d
10. **True.** The high salt levels in the Dead Sea keep people afloat.
11. d

Be Polite Around the Globe, pages 16–17

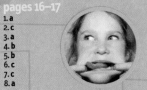

1. a
2. c
3. a
4. b
5. b
6. c
7. c
8. a
9. c
10. **True.** It's considered rude because your host will think that you did not get enough food.
11. **True.** A light handshake is fine, though most people—even in areas of business—kiss each other once on each cheek instead.
12. c
13. d
14. c

Map Mania! Wonders of the World, pages 18–19

1. a
2. c
3. c
4. d
5. c
6. **True.** Inca workers likely used ropes and levers to move heavy stones up the towering mountain.
7. b

Match the Wonder to the Map

8. Taj Mahal-**F-Agra, India**
9. Colosseum-**D-Rome, Italy**
10. Christ the Redeemer Statue-**C-Rio de Janeiro, Brazil**
11. Chichén Itzá-**A-Yucatán, Mexico**
12. Great Wall-**G-stretches an estimated 4,500 miles (7,242 km) across China**
13. Machu Picchu-**B-near Cusco, Peru**
14. Petra-**E-southwest Jordan**

Game Show: Ultimate Global Challenge, pages 20–21

1. c
2. c
3. **False.** The Golden Gate Bridge is painted "international orange."
4. b
5. b
6. c
7. d
8. b
9. b
10. d
11. c
12. **True.** Heart Reef is part of Australia's Great Barrier Reef.
13. a
14. d
15. c

SCORING

0-46

THERE'S NO PLACE LIKE HOME

You may feel most comfortable close to home, but you don't have to go far to explore your world. Try international foods, watch travel shows on television, or make a friend who's from another country. You'll learn more about the world and discover places you may want to visit one day.

47-92

TRAVELER IN TRAINING

You are naturally curious about other countries and cultures. Continue to explore, and before you know it you'll be adding the Wonders of the World to your list of dream vacations!

93-137

EXPLORER EXTRAORDINAIRE

You don't like to let your passport gather dust! You just wish you had a bigger allowance so you could hop a plane to anywhere. Let your travel bug be your guide, and one day you might join the ranks of famous explorers such as Ferdinand Magellan and Marco Polo.